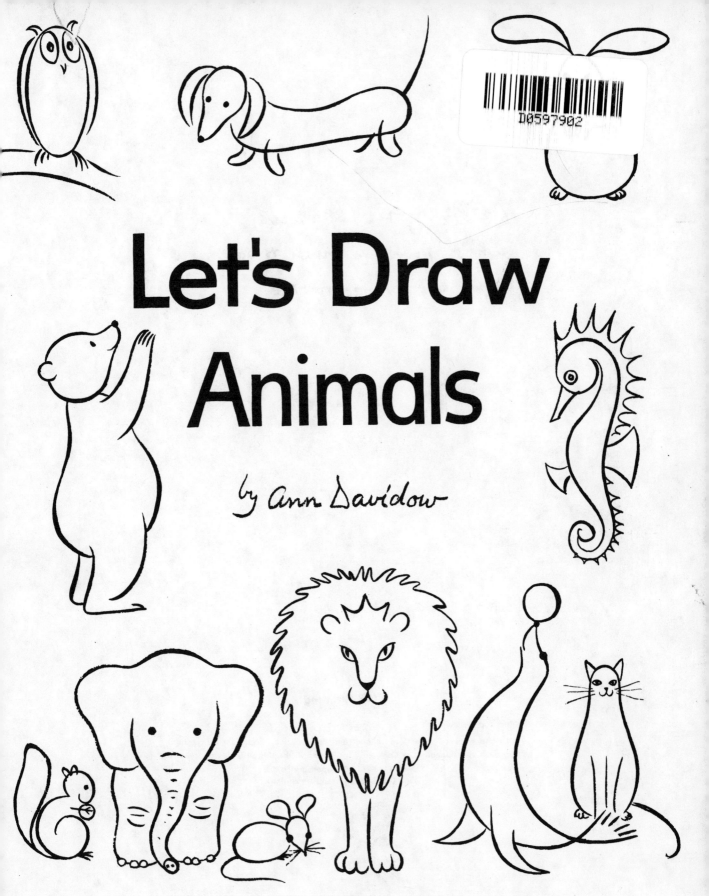

Let's Draw
Animals

by Ann Davidow

GROSSET & DUNLAP • **Publishers** • **NEW YORK**

for Marjorie Barrows,
who's given so much to so many
and even more to me.

1977 Printing

© 1960, by Ann Davidow

All rights reserved under International and Pan-American Copyright Conventions.
Published simultaneously in Canada.   Printed in the United States of America.
ISBN: 0-448-02917-0 (Paperback Edition)
ISBN: 0-448-03326-7 (Library Edition)

INTRODUCTION

Dear Reader:

   Let's Draw Animals is probably best described as a book of drawing games that are to be played for fun. It is fun and it is simple to draw an animal (or anything, for that matter) in steps. Perhaps it is more fun and even simpler if the steps are also tricks. (In this book you will see how to make a whale out of a wave or a seal out of a moon, which is what I mean by "tricks." You will understand how it is done the minute you see the drawings.) The steps and tricks are also set to rhyme.

   I am sure that anyone can see what this book *is*. Perhaps it is more important to explain what it is *not*. It is not a book to teach anyone the best or the only way to draw anything. There are innumerable ways to draw anything; such is the wonder of art. Throughout these pages, I have tried to hint at this truth by suggesting variations. (For example, if you alter the "sheep shapes" a little this way and a little that way, you will cause the sheep to change position before your eyes!)

   None of these drawings is difficult to copy, but if I were watching you, I would not be happy unless I could see that your success with them was encouraging you to try fresh ideas of your own. Imagination, expression and the personal touch are what really count. These can come only from you.

   And, by the way, if you do become an expert at drawing an owl, let us say, I do not think you will be content to leave the poor bird completely up in the air. Just naturally you will want to place him in a picture-world of some kind (perhaps with more owls and other creatures, too). In these pages I have sketched some completed pictures to show you what can be done. Do not copy them, however. Your picture-world should be of your own making.

   If you are a young artist, my fondest hope is that some of the suggestions in this book will start you bounding. But even if *Let's Draw* does not accomplish that, I hope that it will bring a measure of enjoyment. If you have always thought that you couldn't draw at all, perhaps it will give you a little push into the realm of sketching-pleasure.

   Perhaps the best suggestion this book contains is the title all by itself — *Let's Draw*. So . . . let's!

Sincerely,
Ann Davidow

Our mouse's head is like a tear.
A smaller drop can be his ear.

His body, in most any pose,
is simply made by adding O's.

Mice enjoy a bite of cheese

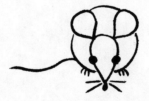

and frightening silly girls at teas.

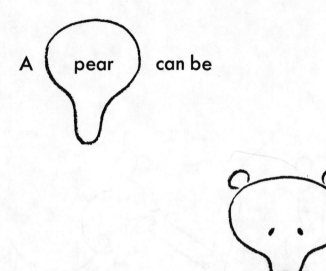

A pear can be

a bear.

A pear can be a horse.

A pear can be

a fox . . . OR . . .

 a pussy cat, of course.

A pear can be  a puppy dog,

and what else can it do?

Is it fair to say a pear
could possibly be you?

SHEEP

Make large and long the letter U,
just the way you always do.

To make a nose, use letter Y;
add V's and dots for ear and eye.

Give him lots of curly wool —
why not give him three bags full?

Draw sheep alone, draw sheep in flocks,
but don't forget their shoes and socks.

PARROT

A curly cane is just the thing

to make a polly on a swing.

Painted polly, can you talk?

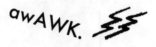 Polly want-a-cracker,

awAWK.

OWL

Draw spectacles
for reading books.

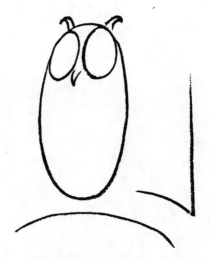

Add one large loop
and three small hooks.

How-de-do?
Whooo are you?
I'm an owl.

To-wit!
To-woo!

SEAL

From a moon let's make a seal,
slippery as banana peel,

with fishy tail
and finny foot

and bouncing ball upon his snoot.

DACHSHUND

From a wiener l o n g and round,

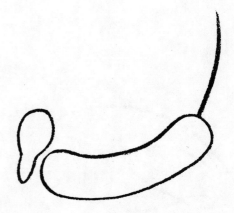

let us make

a little hound.

Draw a number 2 and fit

this wavy squiggle over it.

A few more lines will make a sad
froggy on a lily pad.

To make a froggy from a kite,

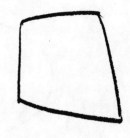

add four plump frog's legs
left and right.

In one big hop

he goes

ker-PLOP!

HEN

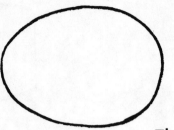

This egg will make a mother hen

and she'll make many eggs again.
There, beneath her feather-fluff,

each will hatch a yellow puff.

ROOSTER

With broken egg shells

make the cock

who's master of
the chicken flock.

17

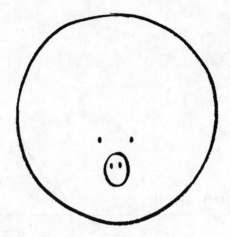

The figure of Madam La Pig
is roly-poly, round and big.

Her toes are pointed, her nose is pug;

she greets you simply by saying, "Ugg!"

She curls her tail to look her best
and lies in mud for a beauty rest.

Though sometimes dirty, sometimes rude,

she's "Mama" to her little brood.

GOAT

Billy boy, the lazy goat,

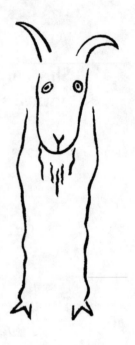

with crooked horn and shaggy coat,

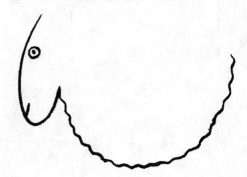

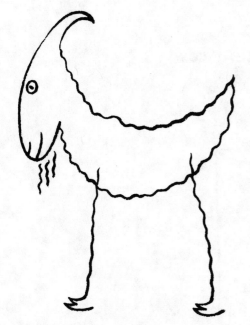

and saggy tum and hairy chin

eats everything from oats to tin.

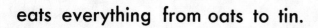

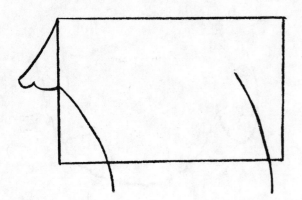

From a box to make a cow

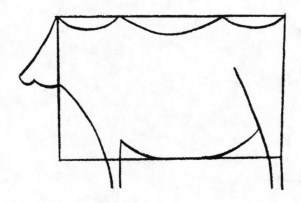

takes just a bit of knowing how.

Draw cows who chew,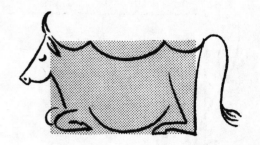

and cows who MOOₒ

and cows who stand and look at you.

DEER

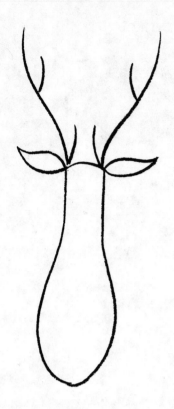

With leaf and branch for horn and ear,

Here's a vase that makes a deer.

Father deer is proud to be
the wearer of the family tree.

DUCKS

D is for duck, a rocking D,

with a touch of filigree.

Draw ducks that do a-waddling go

and ducks that paddle in a row.

SPARROWS

Sparrows, common as the penny,

just as plain and just as many,

are so greedy and so stout,
they crowd the other birdies out.

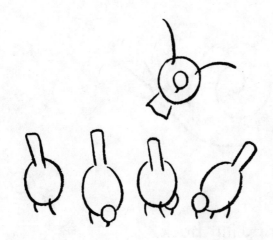

SNAIL

The snail is never far from home.

Where'er he goes, his house will come.

He leaves behind a silver track

so he can go a-rippling back.

BUTTERFLY

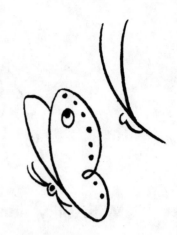

Flutter, flutter,
flutter, flutter,
flutter by,

pretty, pretty,
pretty, pretty,
butterfly.

COCKER SPANIEL

With silky ears and big brown eyes,

he's lovable and very wise.

He does his best to be so cute,
when begging at his master's boot.

POODLE

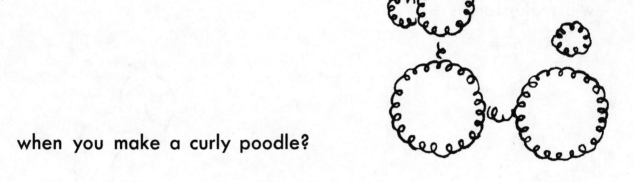

Why not use a circle-doodle

when you make a curly poodle?

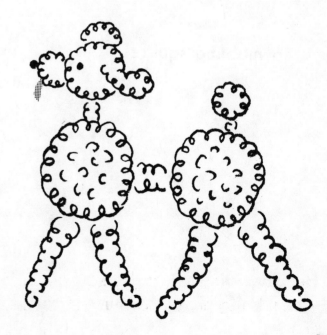

Poodles, full of fun and pomp,
are always ready for a romp.

SQUIRREL

A number 3 with lots of curl
will make for us

a nibbling squirrel.

KOALA BEAR

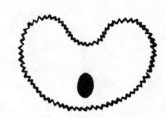

With rounded nose and fuzzy hair,

the koala is a treetop bear.

When baby is too young to climb,
he clings to Mother all the time.

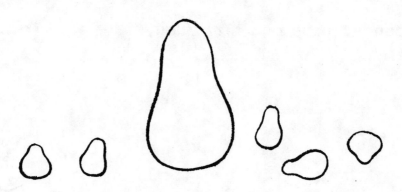

Pears can be hares

with pink in their ears and long, silky whiskers
and cottontail rears.

KITTENS

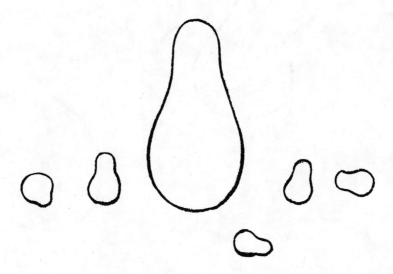

Pears can be kittens

and kittens and kittens,
puffy and fluffy and muffy as mittens.

BEARS

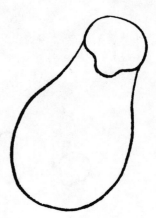

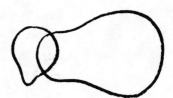

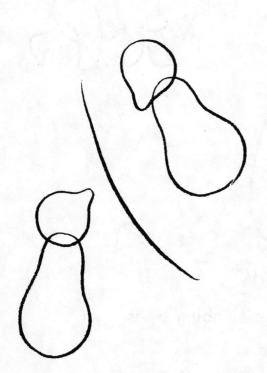

Pears can be bears
(next page, please)—

rolling bears

and strolling bears

and bears a-climbing trees.

HORSES

Pears can be a quiet horse
with a steady gaze.

Pears can be the same horse
with head down to graze.

Side views (with three pears) are also lots of fun —

Make horses trotting,

horses rearing,

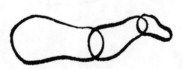

horses on the run.

The beast that has the largest smile,

the evil-grinning crocodile,

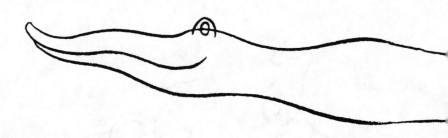

is long and lanky in the lake,

CROCODILE

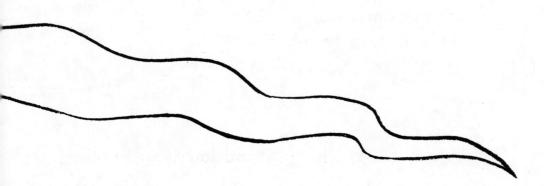

sleepy-looking, yet awake,

hunting for a toothsome treat.

Now who looks good enough to eat?

PORCUPINE

From the flower of a thistle
make a porcupine a-bristle.

Ouch! If he should prickle you,
it surely wouldn't tickle you!

OPOSSUM

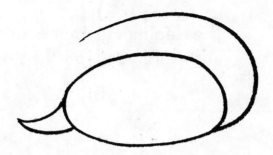

Mama possum's plain and gray,
excepting on a family day,

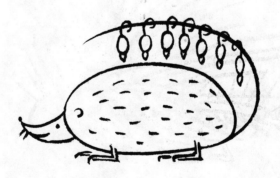

her babies to her tail will cling
like pretty pearls upon a string.

SEA HORSE

The sea horse is the strangest breed—
partly fish and partly steed.

He wears a prickly coat of mail
that covers him from top to tail.

Rearing, bowing so polite,
is he a mermaid's faithful knight?

SWAN

This graceful number 2 will make

a graceful swan upon a lake,

black as night or white as snow,
gliding, gliding, to and fro.

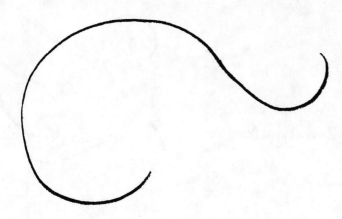

From this wave we get the notion
of a motion in the ocean

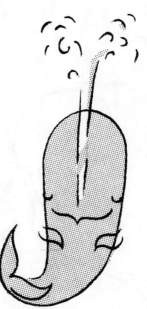

flipping up a giant tail.
It's a fountain-spoutin' whale!

The monkeys think it's quite a joke
that they resemble human folk.

Dangling by their tails and toes
and wearing not a stitch of clothes,

they very often seem to tell us,

"Clumsy people, *you* are jealous!"

CAMEL

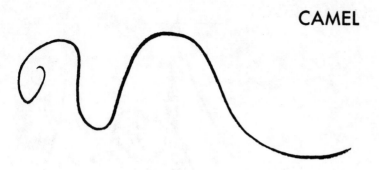

This seems to be a wiggly snake
humping up its back,

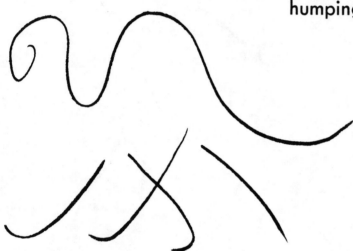

but really, it's a humpy camel
going at a rack.

KANGAROO

Some bouncing lines, and just a few,

will make a bouncing kangaroo.

Although her hops are rather steep,
they rock her baby right to sleep.

GIRAFFE

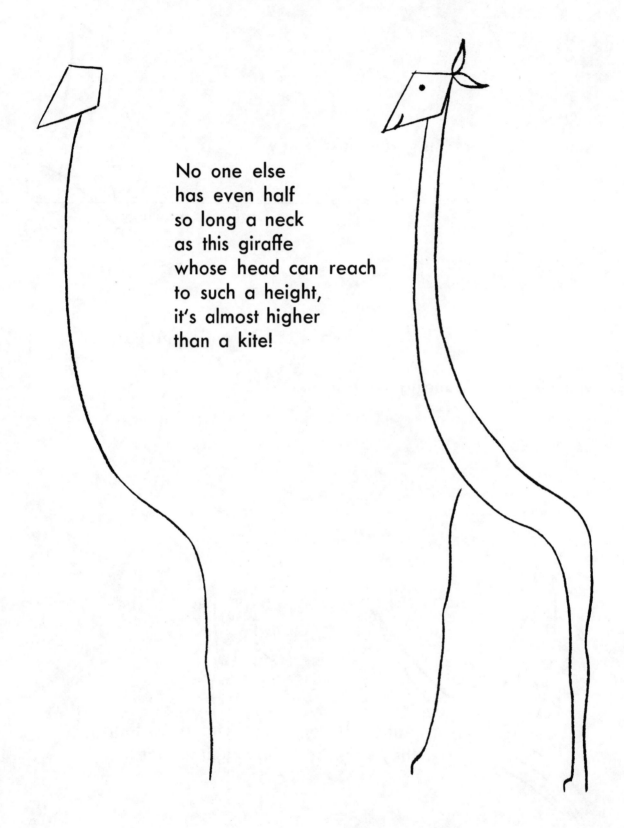

No one else
has even half
so long a neck
as this giraffe
whose head can reach
to such a height,
it's almost higher
than a kite!

Why was he born
with knobby horn
and lots and lots
of funny spots?
And why is he
so lean and slim?
Has somebody
been stretching him?

Can you make turtles out of O 's

hint:

and bunnies out of B 's?

hint:

From QRS , can you make cats,

hint:

and parrots out of  's?

hint:

Can you change (L) two different ways to make a fish or bird?

hint:

And can you make some MWWEe , wee pigs from that funny word?

hint:

answers on pages 78 & 79

LION

Here's the lion's roaring sound.

Let's make of it a ring around the lion's face
so it is plain

that he's a king with mighty mane.

TIGER

Why does the tiger not complain,
"I wish *I* had a mighty mane"?

Because he has what lions lack:

handsome stripes of gold and black.

WALRUS

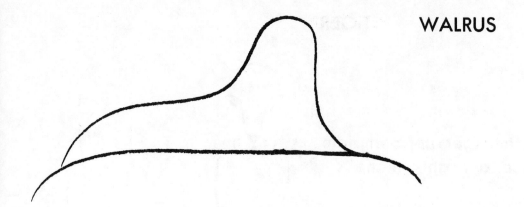

The walrus thinks it's very nice

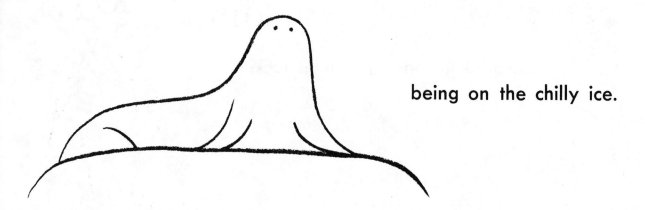

being on the chilly ice.

There he sits upon his fins

grinning goofus-toofus grins.

PENGUIN

Here's a pair of bowling tenpins.

 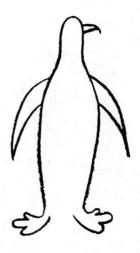

Here's a pair of strolling penguins.

They're the birds with most finesse because they wear tuxedo dress.

From a stuffy little stool,

make a beast that's hard and cruel.

He'll never be a friend to us,
the cranky old rhinoceros.

HIPPOPOTAMUS

This ball-on-legs begins for us

a hefty hippopotamus.

"Hippopotamus" is, of course,
a fancy word for water-horse.

PEACOCK

An "eye" will make the peacock's head

Around it, many more are spread.

No other bird can so surprise you
with a tail that really eyes you!

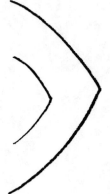

On silver fins
that barely swish,

gently swim
the angelfish.

In the blue of sunlight seas,
they glide about in twos and threes.

ELEPHANT

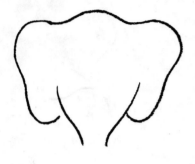

Draw a funny little plant.
Could *this* be an elephant?

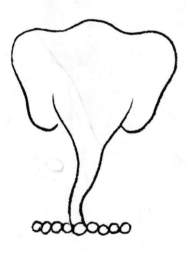

It has a trunk
(like Jumbo's nose)
and 'round it rocks
(that might be toes).

So add two tusks and add two knees

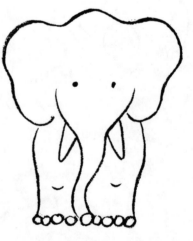

and here are Jumbos in the trees!

DINOSAUR

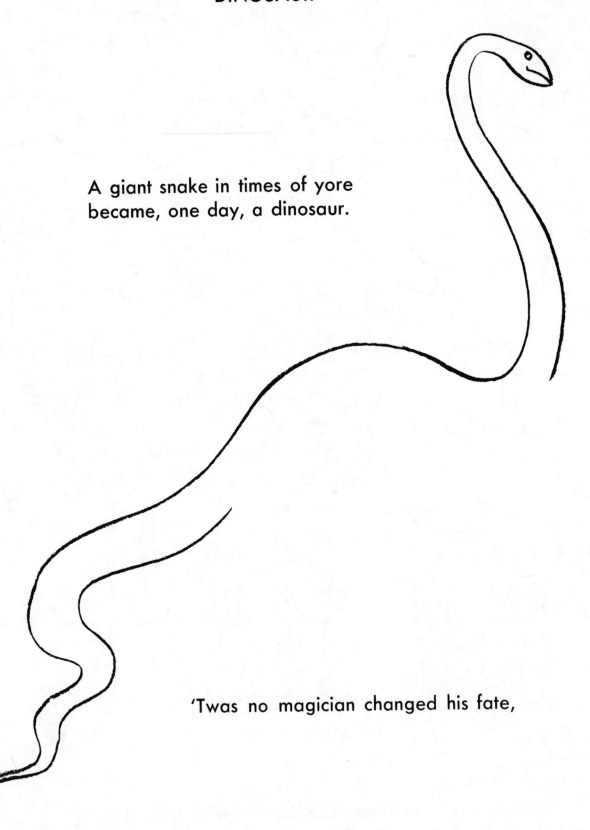

A giant snake in times of yore
became, one day, a dinosaur.

'Twas no magician changed his fate,

but just that elephant he ate.

THE FANTASTIC GARDEN

The seven pages that follow contain suggestions for drawing mythical beasts

CENTAUR

The Centaur, who lived long ago,
was man above

        and horse below.

The man in him thought it was fun
to run as fast as horses run.

(continued on the next page)

The horse in him thought it was grand
to have a human head and hand.

We live in other times, of course,
when man is man and horse is horse!

UNICORN

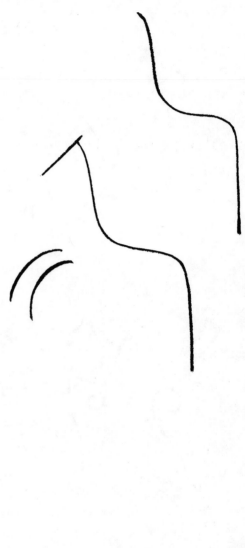

The Unicorn, by way of note,
was partly horse and partly goat,

But, since he had a single horn,
was rightly called the "Uni-corn."

The Griffin was the strangest thing.

He had an eagle's head and wing,

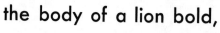

the body of a lion bold,

and, for a tail, a snake of gold.

PHOENIX

"Splendid" is the only word
that could describe the Phoenix-bird

with sparkling diamonds in his crest
and ruby feathers on his breast

Splendid!

Like the flaming sun,
the world has never known

        but one.

THE FANTASTIC GARDEN

Once, in an ancient garden spot,
Lived creatures that today are not.
Centaurs carried pipe and flute
And little arrows they could shoot
At Unicorns who, just for fun,
Would sometimes butt at them and run.
Griffins bold protected all
From enemies who came to call,
Till Phoenix had a strange desire:
He beat his wings and burst afire!
This happy land became forthwith
A heap of ashes and a myth.

(the picture is *just to look at*)

THE FANTASTIC GARDEN

Turtles out of O's

Bunnies out of B's

Kitties out of QRS

Parrots out of p's

Little L becomes a fish

and then becomes a bird

and here we've made a MWWEe, wee pig
from that funny word!

OCTOPUS

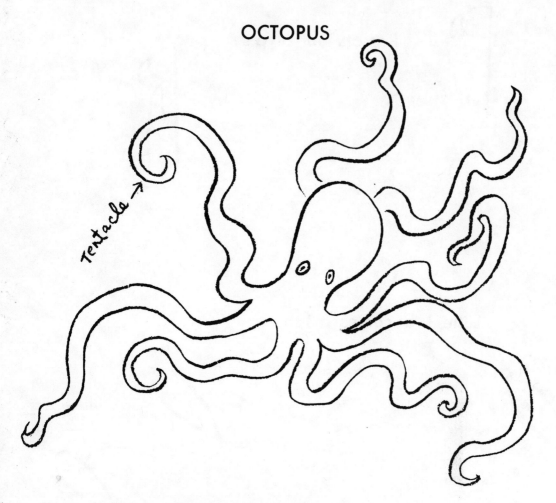

Hercules*, the octopus,
Is raising quite an awful fuss
By wriggling his identicals
(Those higgledy-piggledy tentacles).
How quickly all his friends are gone—
They know he means the squeeze is on!

*Hercules = strong man